THE MYSTERY
of
SILBURY HILL

WHY WAS IT BUILT?

Published in 2005 by
Elar Publishing

All photographs by the author

Illustrations by D. Slater

Edited by N. J. Watkins BA

Printed in Great Britain by
Cromwell Press, Trowbridge, Wiltshire

ISBN
0-9551567-0-X
978-0-9551567-0-0

To Cecile

1923 – 2003

CONTENTS

APPENDIX

INDEX

LIST OF ILLUSTRATIONS

INTRODUCTION

The Wiltshire landscape, the Marlborough Downs and Salisbury Plain are unique. For centuries writers have been inspired by the sheer simplicity of the gently rolling chalklands stretching into the far distance.

It is a most distinctive scenery with endless open skies, a touch of romance and a special historical heritage unequalled in the British Isles. Stone circles and burial mounds, huge stone structures and deep ditches, ancient trackways and field systems are scattered across the Downs.

Reality and fact have gradually blended in with the folklore and legends which surround the many remains of those ancient monuments on the windswept uplands.

There they are, steeped in mystery and magic, the guardians of the distant past, their true meaning and purpose having been somewhat lost in the mist of time.

A well established and organised population must have existed to provide the considerable manpower required for the construction of the many monuments which are believed by some to be a centre of the Neolithic religion.

The Sanctuary, the West Kennett Long Barrow and the West Kennett palisade enclosures, plus the building of stone-lined avenues, stone circles and deep ditches at Avebury are probably all interconnected by the religious beliefs of the Neolithic people. They are visible and lasting evidence of gigantic efforts to pay tribute to Mother Earth the Great Goddess, the Universal Provider and other visions which regulated and dominated all aspects of the lives of the Neolithic people.

Only Silbury Hill stands aside. The huge mound does not fit readily into a pattern, into the mosaic of Neolithic rituals and tradition. Furthermore, the time frame in which it was built is a rather grey area relative to other monuments on the Downs whose precise construction dates are also surrounded by a bewildering array of figures, contradictions and doubts. In consequence we close our eyes and minds and believe in what we want to believe. Nevertheless, many questions and unsolved mysteries remain.

It may seem at times as if our distant ancestors created the various structures and monuments merely to produce a puzzle for those that followed on. Silbury Hill has to be seen and evaluated against such background of confusion.

SILBURY HILL

Silbury Hill, near Avebury by the the side of the A4 road on the Marlborough Downs, was built approximately 4600 years ago in the Neolithic period *(Fig. 1)*. The age has now been tentatively confirmed by many excavations that have taken place over the years.

Fig. 1 *A dramatic view of Silbury Hill as the road sweeps over the brow of Waden Hill.*

However, precise details of its exact age vary and are still rather sketchy. There is also the strong possibility that the construction of Silbury Hill was out of sheer necessity a simultaneous event with the building of other structures in the vicinity which put a tremendous strain on the communities and their resources.

Some may say without doubt that Silbury Hill must rank as one of the greatest unsolved mysteries of prehistoric times perhaps only overshadowed by the ongoing saga of the 'Blue Stones' within the Stonehenge monument which were either transported by man or by glaciation from the Preseli Mountains in Wales.

It may seem strange that Silbury Hill, the largest artificial mound in Europe, was not built on lofty, commanding heights where its presence would be obvious from afar to deter marauders and invaders. Instead it occupies relatively low and very often waterlogged ground in the valley by the infant River Kennet or, as some may prefer to call it, the Winterbourne.

Part of the hill, some 38 m above ground level and 168 m across its base, can be seen from the nearby Sanctuary and also from the West Kennett Long Barrow. Only the very top of the hill is visible above Waden Hill from the Ridgeway *(Fig. 2)*. Rather surprisingly, it cannot be seen from the Avebury stone circles nor from the West Kennett Avenue leading up to the Sanctuary, a short distance to the north.

Fig. 2   *Only the top of Silbury Hill (arrow) can be seen from the Ridgeway to the east. During the Neolithic era the hill would not have been visible due to the extensive tree cover on the Downs.*

The most distant views, but still rather limited, are from Milkhill, Cherhill, Windmill Hill and from the top of the Calne and Devizes roads converging on Beckhampton from the west. Due to its rather low position good views of Silbury Hill are much restricted today. This was even more the case in Neolithic times when the hill was partly or completely hidden by dense woodland in the immediate vicinity and by an extensive covering of trees on the uplands. To a casual observer from afar the hill would not have been visible.

Over the years many suggestions have been advanced and much exploratory work has been carried out by sinking a shaft from above to the base of the mound and by tunnelling at various times into the sides and the centre of the hill to discover the purpose of such a monumental undertaking, but to no avail. Cutting a series of trenches on the outside and advanced seismic surveys in bore holes also failed to provide a conclusive answer *(Fig. 26 & Fig. 27)*.

The hill was not yielding its secrets, if indeed it contained any, and somehow every generation added a little more to that already existing mysterious and legendary past. Maybe it was meant to be a beacon, a sign of a territorial statement or a look-out to warn of pending attacks. On reflection this would not be a very plausible scenario as visibility was severely restricted by the surrounding terrain.

Fig. 3 *The view from Waden Hill to the north shows the low position of Silbury Hill within the*
Chalk Downs. Water from the springs surrounds the base of the hill. Note the exposed upper
terrace as well as the slight bulge on the right-hand side of the hill due to soil creep.

Or was it perhaps built to be a fortification, a means of defence? But these are put on top of
natural hills commanding a wide view of the area. The adjacent Waden Hill, its height being
slightly above the top of Silbury Hill, might have proved a better location *(Fig. 3)*. In any
case what was there to defend? A hill which was situated in the middle of a marshy,
waterlogged area for most of the year? The nearest settlements were at Avebury a short
distance to the north and an attacker would have simply bypassed the hill leaving those on
the relatively small area on top completely isolated. That the base of the mound was in part
surrounded by water throughout the year was unlikely to be meant as a deterrent since there
was a broad causeway allowing easy access to the hill from the chalk spur to the south.
Nevertheless, because the hill was there, the 30 m wide flat top was used for a short time as
a Saxon fort in the 11th century to protect, no doubt, the then much-used original Roman
road skirting the hill. A clump of trees adorned the top at a later stage.

Neolithic tradition does not favour the idea of a burial mound either when one considers
that the hill was in part surrounded by a 9 m deep water-filled ditch spreading out into an
extensive and at that time a relatively deep lake to the west. All the burial mounds and
barrows of the Neolithic era are on top of natural, dry ground and not within a low, wet and
marshy environment. Although the ditch has now silted up, the area is still waterlogged after
heavy rainfall.

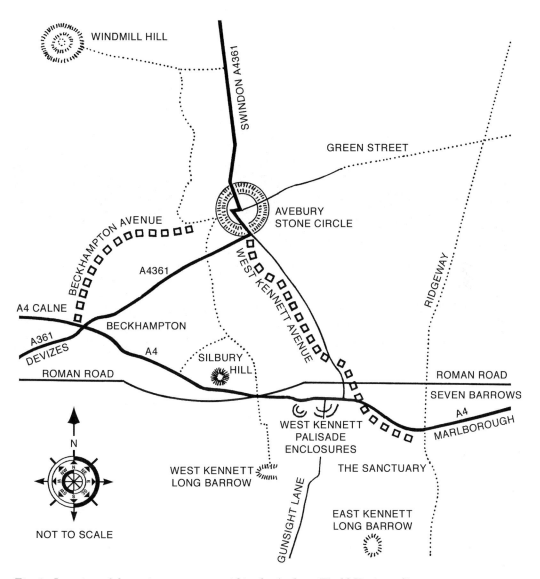

WINDMILL HILL

SWINDON A4361

GREEN STREET

AVEBURY
STONE CIRCLE

BECKHAMPTON AVENUE

A4361

WEST KENNETT AVENUE

RIDGEWAY

A4 CALNE

A361
DEVIZES

BECKHAMPTON

A4

SILBURY
HILL

ROMAN ROAD

ROMAN ROAD

SEVEN BARROWS

A4
MARLBOROUGH

WEST KENNETT
PALISADE
ENCLOSURES

THE SANCTUARY

N

WEST KENNETT
LONG BARROW

GUNSIGHT LANE

EAST KENNETT
LONG BARROW

NOT TO SCALE

Fig. 4 *Location of the main monuments within the Avebury World Heritage Site.*

It is worth noting that evidence of a burial has indeed been found on top of the hill but it was certainly not primary and does not help in solving the meaning and purpose of Silbury Hill.

Added to such confusion are the results of radiocarbon dating from flora and soil samples and from the very few artifacts recovered during excavations within the hill. The actual dates fluctuate wildly, whether relative to the hill itself, the other monuments in the surrounding area or within the context of the Neolithic period *(Fig. 4)*. They are of little help in placing Silbury Hill or even the duration of construction into a precise time window. Taking all the available data into consideration a date of 2300 to 3000 years BC is a reasonable assumption.

Fig. 5 *View from the south also emphasizes the low position of Silbury Hill built at the foot of the sloping chalk promontory. Trees in the immediate surroundings and on lower ground during Neolithic times would have obscured the existence of the hill.*

The hill consists of 350,000 cubic metres of chalk and soil, but only 250,000 cubic metres had actually been dug out in its construction. The volume difference between these two figures is due to the local topography.

The megalith builders quarried into a sloping chalk promontory *(Fig. 5)* shaping part of it into a steep sided conical base to provide a stable foundation for the greater part of the hill which was built on top of two pre-existing earlier, but smaller, mounds.

This in effect meant that by utilising the natural elevated contours of the surrounding land they only had to build up 29 m of material to produce a hill standing 37 m above ground level. Exact measurements vary considerably from record to record but modern research suggests a height of only 37 m.

The final height of their project appears to have been of little importance, even completely irrelevant. Had they wanted height, the ancient builders could have exploited any of the commanding positions of the adjacent natural elevations to a much greater effect.

The building of Silbury Hill was a gigantic task by any standards even though chalk was a relatively easy material to work. But was it really that unusual? Perhaps not.

During the construction of an 18 m deep trench around the Avebury stone circles, probably tens of years or more before the Silbury structure, a massive 130,000 cubic metres of chalk and soil were removed and heaped up into a bank around the edge of the excavated ditch area. The amount of material removed was roughly more than half of that quarried for Silbury Hill.

Further evidence of their ability to work with enormous quantities of chalk are the many prominent barrows and burial mounds in the immediate landscape. Digging deep ditches and moving huge amounts of chalk for large scale projects appeared to have been a way of life for Neolithic man on the Chalk Downs. Within such a context the building of Silbury Hill loses some of its mystery and apparent great significance.

So, why was Silbury Hill built? What was its purpose? Why indeed was it built upon two already existing earlier mounds and a small central core? And why can the hill not be seen from the sacred and unique Avebury stone circles and the stone lined Avenue?

Stripping away the mysterious aura, legends, folklore and the sometimes bizarre ideas regarding the purpose of Silbury Hill the local geology may provide a decisive clue and possibly a straightforward answer.

THE IMPORTANCE OF WATER

Chalklands are by their very nature relatively dry areas. Any rain soaks quickly into the permeable rocks leaving little or no surface water or run-off, but chalk rock is not as uniform in its texture as it may appear at first glance.

There are many irregular clay, marl and hard chalk bands at various horizons within the Chalk as well as large fissures and joints. The Melbourn Rock is one such feature. It forms a layer of an exceptionally hard chalkstone, one to three metres thick within the chalk.

Below the Melbourn Rock lies a thin layer of sticky green clay known as Plenus Marl, after the fossils it contains. These clay layers have the effect of inhibiting free downward percolation of rainwater after it has slowly worked its way through the porous rock. The water is trapped and builds up to form aquifers, huge underground reservoirs. The top of these is known as the water table.

Depending on the time of year the height of the water table varies within the rock. Water will flow readily out in any direction where the water table intersects the ground surface. Springs will emerge in such places forming the springline either at the foot of the chalk escarpment, or higher up, above an impermeable clay or marl horizon.

The movement of water within the chalk is extremely slow. It can take from one to three months, after periods of precipitation, to increase the height of the water table within the aquifer for springs to emerge. Some of these springs are very active and may flow throughout the year with varying amounts of water, whilst others are rather irregular or have significant lower rates of flow depending on seasonal rainfall or indeed unusual or cyclical climatic variations.

It was water, and above all the ready and constant availability of water, which attracted Neolithic man to the otherwise dry chalklands and finally dictated his way of life in the solitude of the Downs. With the passing of time settlements and communities rapidly expanded and farming stock increased as more of the wild woodland was cleared from the coombes and uplands around Avebury.

The very success and existence of Neolithic man on the chalklands depended more and more on defined seasons and a steady, unchanging climate to guarantee the substantial and continuous availability of water to sustain an increased farming and population growth.

In the normal course of events such life giving water, so important for man and beast alike, came from the many springs and streams draining into the vales and lower lying land. One of these, and the only one of some consequence, is the seasonal Winterbourne stream which rises at the foot of the chalk escarpment in Uffcot, south of Wroughton, forming a pond not unlike a huge dewpond.

The Winterbourne stream then winds its way through Winterbourne Bassett, Berwick Bassett and Winterbourne Monkton, its strength during wet seasons being boosted by numerous smaller streams from the chalk uplands to the east. It continues towards Avebury where it is joined by the Yatesbury Brook. The flow of water is further increased by several large springs downstream from Avebury where the Winterbourne becomes the River Kennet at the Swallowhead Springs on its journey towards Marlborough.

There is some difference of opinion here. Some are adamant that it is the Kennet which rises at Uffcot and the Winterbourne, a seasonal chalk stream, is merely a name for the upper reaches of the Kennet. For convenience and clarity only the name Kennet will be used throughout the following text.

Today, the water table has been lowered because of climatic conditions and continuous extraction by the water authorities. All the springs dry up at certain times of the year and long stretches of the upper Kennet are completely dry for long periods.

This is in stark contrast to the vastly different conditions in the Avebury area some 5000 years ago before Silbury Hill was built *(Fig. 6)*. There was always an abundant supply of water throughout the year from the wetlands in the vicinity and also from many springs in the immediate area, the Swallowhead, Waden Hill and Silbury springs, as well as from the Beckhampton and Fir Tree springs and many others. Some were seasonal, others flowed throughout the year.

There were no well-defined streams like the Kennet, the Beckhampton stream and the Yatesbury Brook of today, but many streamlets which meandered across the shallow expanse of wooded wetland in the Avebury area shifting their courses from season to season leaving an intertwined, array of shallow river channels which extended downstream well beyond the area of the present Silbury Hill site. Such abundance of water drained through a relatively narrow but swampy, waterlogged area at the foot of Waden Hill towards the broad floodplain of West Overton.

The settlements on the gentle rolling chalklands around Avebury were well established. Forest clearance on an ever-increasing scale on the uplands provided sufficient arable land for their needs. Pasture land and grazing were clearly of importance to the Neolithic people. The seasons were constant and predictable; water for man and beast was in plentiful supply. Life of the ancient people revolved around their Gods and tribute was paid to whatever other powers they believed in.

CLIMATE CHANGE

The very existence and survival of the growing communities on the Downs depended entirely on the availability of water in ever increasing quantities to supply all their needs. Towards the end of the Neolithic period climate change was looming on the horizon. A climate phase known as the 'Sub-boreal' with irregular and extremely long, dry periods was overshadowing the activities of the Neolithic people and their constructions on the Chalk Downs *(Fig. 29)*.

It was also a timely reminder that they were living on a restless, moving planet where never anything stands still – be it their physical surroundings or the vagaries of a turbulent climate. The Neolithic people where in constant struggle with their environment. The world is a place of continuous change – always has been – always will be. The settlements on the Avebury Downs faced a challenge for survival.

Unusual dry seasons in some years affected the output from many springs in the area. The flow of water stopped at times or became intermittent or was so reduced in volume during certain periods that it was insufficient to satisfy the demands of the people living and farming on the dry chalklands.

Lack of water may have been worse in some years than in others. Prolonged seasonal droughts became longer and more frequent. However, climate change is not an immediate process. It straddles across the boundaries of long periods with varying consequences. Gradually the pendulum swung in the opposite direction. Where once there were springs continuously bubbling from deep within the chalk hills flowing into streams, marshland and water meadows, there was now an increasing lack of water at certain times of the year.

Dried up springs meant no water, and water for man and beast alike was not within reach elsewhere. Neolithic man on the parched Downs was confronted by a looming climatic catastrophe. Sufficient rainfall and dependable seasons were no longer a certainty. His survival depended entirely upon the availability of water.

Rainfall well below average and considerably higher temperatures caused gradual lowering of the water table and drying of the top soil. Increasingly frequent warm, gale-force winds blowing across the parched Downs were taking with them the thin and once fertile soil cover from precious, newly-cultivated farmland.

Evidence of such arid and turbulent climatic conditions in the late Neolithic period can be seen in the dusty infillings of the 'Y' and 'Z' holes which may have been the previous setting of the 'Blue Stones' inside the Stonehenge monument. Similar localised wind deposits of red loam have been found in soil layers within the base of timber post holes and stones guarding the entrances to barrows and burial mounds.

Neolithic settlements on higher ground became gradually uninhabited possibly due to the shortage of water. Population growth declined. Nature slowly reclaimed the cultivated fields. Silence reigned in finally-abandoned upper chalkland settlements. That part of the Neolithic period is sometimes referred to in some records as the 'Dark Age' in the prehistory of southern Britain.

Detailed insect, seed, pollen and molluscan analysis shows a distinct change from a swampy environment to much drier conditions in the Kennet vale south of Avebury. In a comparatively short time, grassland invaded the once permanently waterlogged areas.

Peat bogs in southern England were also drying up at the same time. The waters were draining away. Boats could no longer be used to move around the wetlands. Trackways had to be built across the muddy, soft ground. The once wet and marshy areas were gradually replaced by forests of pine and yew. A peat bog surface is very sensitive to climate change. One of such *'standstill phases'* in peat growth during the Neolithic period and subsequent renewed growth known as *'recurrence surfaces'* are clearly recorded within the alternating moorland deposits on the Somerset Levels and throughout English bogs.

A contributing and very often overlooked factor in the changing environment was the rapid clearance of ancient woodland and shrub cover in the vales and on the uplands by Neolithic farmers to gain more land for cultivation.

In due course, more and more ground had to be cleared to replace the thin soil cover lost to constant wind erosion during long periods of extremely dry conditions. In consequence, the ever-increasing evaporation rate would have, at times, overtaken the already diminishing rainfall and contributed to the ongoing lowering of the water table.

There are many factors and variables which may have caused a severe climate change during the Neolithic period. The last major ice age had just finished. Ice sheets and glaciers were melting as the earth warmed up. Sea levels rose having a direct effect on ocean currents and in consequence influencing the general climatic pattern which was periodically oscillating wildly from one extreme to the other.

The interaction between the forces of nature, atmosphere, ice and sea are extremely complex. The net result was a warmer and much drier climate even though such changes may not always correlate with the weather pattern in other parts of Europe at that particular time. However, climate change was nothing new. Climatic variability and relative instability of local climate have been in existence throughout the Earth's history right up to present day and is not just confined to the Neolithic period in Britain.

The most puzzling aspect for Neolithic people on the chalklands would have been the fact that most of the springs in the area maintained a much reduced output during or immediately after a wet period but suddenly became more active during a normal dryer period when streams began to flow again, albeit with a rather limited volume. Since there had always been sufficient water for their needs in the past they did not realize that in their now-changing environment rainfall can take up to three months to permeate through the chalk and replenish the aquifers and raise the water table enough to maintain the constant output from the springs in the swampy, marshy vales.

Climatic fluctuations produced exceptionally long dry periods in some years but not in others when there was again sufficient water to sustain the growing communities on the Chalk Downs. Somehow, the Neolithic people, moving away from being hunter-gatherers, had to adapt to such sporadic climate changes in order to ensure their survival. A way had to be found to collect and store water from the springs to ensure a constant supply throughout the year.

THE BIRTH OF SILBURY HILL.
THE CENTRAL CORE

The customs of the Neolithic people living on the Downs appears to have revolved around circular structures as shown by previous constructions in the area. A trench or shallow trough along such lines to serve as a reservoir may have seemed the obvious answer. The location chosen, probably the only and most suitable under the circumstances, was the relatively narrow floodplain west of Waden Hill between the present river Kennet to the north and the projecting chalk spur to the south *(Fig. 6)*.

Fig. 6 *The wooded and marshy area 5000 years ago, before Silbury Hill was built in a hollow near fast flowing springs.*

This particular site was also at the confluence of the once most vigorous group of springs reduced at that time to often intermittent and much diminished outflow. Prolonged dry periods on an ever-increasing scale favoured the invasion of pastureland on the formerly wet and marshy, but now often completely dried-up valley floor. The lowest part of the wooded vale with an insignificant trickle of water, accumulating from time to time from the nearby Silbury springs, was cleared and enclosed by a staked wattle fence. Work commenced by digging a roughly circular shallow trough into the valley floor at the outside of the fence. The excavated material consisting of grass, moss, river gravels and clay with flints was then deposited in the middle of the enclosure forming a small layered mound some 20 m wide and about 1 m high. This is referred to now as the 'Central Core' *(Fig. 7)*. The excavated area was deep enough to reach the water table and also large enough to collect sufficient water for their needs into such an improvised reservoir.

Fig. 7 *The 'Central Core' marked the birth of Silbury Hill. A surrounding wattle fence prevented the material being washed back on to the valley floor and into the scooped-out trench during wet periods. The finished mound was covered with turves.*

At that point in time the structure was meant to be a permanent feature in the vale. The staked wattle fence was put up to prevent erosion once the area became waterlogged again in the lowest parts of the vale during subsequent wetter seasons. There was no intention on the part of the builders to extend or enlarge the hill otherwise they would not have stabilised such a small mound.

This marks the birth of Silbury Hill even though, and this is most significant from the evidence of its construction, the final shape and size we see today was not the intention of the builders at that time. Such simple but absolutely essential beginnings of the infant Silbury Hill also spawned many strange stories, legends, intriguing mysteries and fanciful explanations surrounding the origin and significance of the hill.

SILBURY HILL – PHASE ONE

The changing climate dictated the building of Silbury Hill. Constant availability of water throughout the year was the deciding factor for the initial and subsequent stages of its construction. Silbury Hill was born out of sheer necessity to ensure the survival of the Neolithic communities on the Chalk Downs.

Fig. 8   *The layered, shallow curved mound of 'Phase One' covered the original wattle-fenced*
Central Core. Each layer was covered with turves to be removed again for the subsequent
layer as the trench was deepened. Chalk blocks and Sarsen stones stabilized the layers at
ground level to reduce erosion during intermittent periods of wetter conditions in the vale.

With the passage of time a lower water table within the chalk necessitated digging a wider and deeper trench further out from the original mound to provide a continuous supply of water. To retain the level of water in the surrounding trench, it had to be deep enough to reach the water table which at that time was probably only two or three metres below the surface. If not, any accumulated water would have quickly disappeared again into the porous chalk. The technique of lining the shallow trough with a layer of clay to retain sufficient water above the water table was not known to the Neolithic people even though silting up during wetter seasons would have unintentionally lined the bottom of such a trench.

The excavated material was placed in several successive layers of soil, chalk, river gravels and a mixture of turves on top of the original wattle-fenced structure, covering it completely, and forming a relatively gently curved but very much enlarged mound some 35 m in diameter and approximately 6 m high.

Numerous Sarsen stones and chalk blocks placed around the base in addition to a final upper layer of turves protected the hill from erosion during wetter periods. Although only a few Sarsen stones were located during recent excavations one can safely speculate that they were placed at regular intervals around the base at not only at this particular phase of the construction, but also during the subsequent phase.

The Sarsen stones were obtained from the immediate vicinity and may also have been recovered from just below the surface when digging the trenches. Sarsen stones were, and still are, in abundance on the Downs and in the vales. They appear to be of no special significance other than being a functional component of the completed structure. Their presence might even have proved a hindrance during excavation. The Sarsen stones and their seemingly inappropriate presence on the Chalk Downs is fully described in the appendix of this book along with chalk and flints.

Once again the mound was meant to be a stabilised stand-alone structure without the intention of further enlargement. The builders had completed their task with a sense of purpose and finality. This part of the construction including the initial wattle-fenced central core is referred to as the 'Primary mound', or 'Phase One' *(Fig. 8)*. It is known from tunnelling excavations carried out during 1969/70 that it was summer when the central core within Phase One was heaped up, but there were few other clues as to the meaning and purpose of the final structure.

The organic material and seasonal insects and flora from the site were surprisingly well preserved in the central core. The grass was closely cropped with square ends indicating grazing when the turves were dug from the floor of the normally waterlogged, but then completely dried up vale.

Land snails indicate a dry, well established and open grassland environment. Ants still had their wings ready to fly. Moss was also present in large quantities even though it does not normally grow within a permanently wet environment but on the fringes. Inadvertently such finds provided proof of extremely long dry periods and the hitherto unrecognized severe water shortage at that time.

Radiocarbon dating for some of the material within the central core came from very young and also more mature deposits on the grassland valley floor and therefore fall within a very broad range. They are of little value in dating the initial construction of the hill or successive phases.

The water-level in the scooped out area surrounding the mound of Phase One was dependent on the output from the springs controlled by the height of the fluctuating water table. If the level of the water table dropped below the depth of their excavations, the stored water would quickly disappear again during drier periods when it was most needed.

Due to the vagaries of the climate it became apparent that the size of the initial trench area of Phase One was just not deep or wide enough to tap into the groundwater supply to collect and store sufficient water throughout the drier periods.

SILBURY HILL – PHASE TWO

Another deeper trench, 7 m deep and 14 m wide, was dug further out from the first trench. The excavated material was stacked up in distinct layers inside the enclosed trench area on top of the existing earlier mound of Phase One to construct a second mound approx. 75 m wide at the base.

Fig. 9   *'Phase Two' covering both the Central Core and Phase One. Chalk blocks and probably also some Sarsen stones were again used to stabilize the lower section. The finished mound was covered with turves which were removed from Phase One as excavations of the trench progressed.*

This part of the construction, some 20 m high and known as 'Phase Two', *(Fig. 9)* was already more than half of the final height of the hill we see today. The layers were systematically stabilised with a hard chalk, the 'Melbourn Rock', to prevent erosion and material sliding back into the dug out area. Any Sarsen stones dug up whilst excavating the trench would have also been utilised.

As the trench was deepened to reach the water table during drier seasons another stabilised layer was added. Each layer in turn representing a definite time gap between deposits. Here again the thorough stabilisation and layered construction of the mound indicates finalisation of the task in hand. However, this trench too was not deep enough to compensate for, and reach down, to the now very unpredictable levels of the water table at certain times of the year.

There is some evidence that trial pits and trenches were dug into the original land surface to ascertain the depth of the disappearing water table after completing Phase One and also Phase Two. There appear to be dumps of excavated chalk and clay with flints located at the base of the first mound (Phase One) and subsequent mound (Phase Two).

SILBURY HILL – PHASE THREE

The search for water, once so plentiful throughout the year, dictated the way of life for the rapidly expanding communities on top of the Marlborough Downs. Drier climate and the demand for more water necessitated a still larger storage area or even a permanent small lake on the floor of the vale. Baffled by the irregular flow of the springs, especially the delay after heavy rainfall, the Neolithic workers may have decided to find the source of the water bubbling forth into the sunlight. They may have come to the conclusion that there must be a huge water reservoir deep within the chalk.

Another, but still deeper, trench was dug some 30 metres away from the base of the existing hill, (Phase Two), to allow for extra material to be placed into the enclosed central area should this prove necessary if the trench had to be deepened still further in the future. The builders learned from the construction of the first mound, (Phase One), that the deeper the trench, the higher the hill, the larger the base has to be. So they allowed for any enlargement of the mound.

The floor diameter of the existing mound was increased to approximately 168 m by depositing the excavated material as six well defined steps or benches 4 m to 5 m high on top of each other over the already constructed mounds of the first and second phase. Each upper layer, having a smaller diameter than the one immediately below was thus producing a hill in the shape of a stepped cone 38 m high. This final work is known as 'Phase Three' *(Fig. 10)*.

The three construction phases including the initial central core have been confirmed by several excavations and detailed examinations.

More than half of the total material used to build the hill came from the projecting spur of natural chalkland on the southern side reaching down into the once marshy, waterlogged vale, which was, and still is, the confluence of several streams and numerous springs. The remainder came from the 9 m deep and 38 m wide trench surrounding part of the mound and from a broad, basin-like extension to the main trench leading towards the foot of Waden Hill and the gentle slopes immediately to the east and west of the hill.

Thus a rectangular and deliberate closed-in water storage area, resembling a reservoir or lake, extending some 40 m to 160 m from the base of the hill was created. This was finally sufficient to provide a continuous supply of water from the frequently fluctuating water table levels above the Plenus Marl and Melbourn Rock within the chalk hills.

The final part of the hill with its six defined terraces, suitably stabilized with hard chalk blocks, and the basin-like extension to the west and north was not built as one uninterrupted project without any breaks. The time interval between the various stages and sections would have depended entirely on the vagaries of the climate.

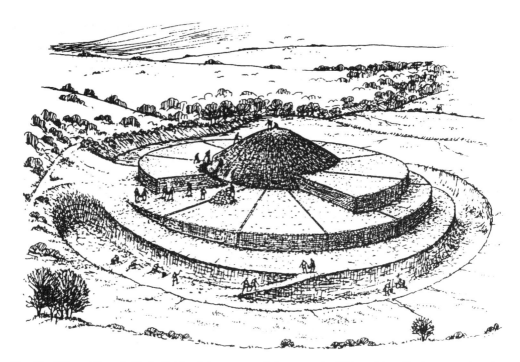

Fig. 10 *'Phase Three'. Six individual tiers covered the mound of Phase Two. Each tier and each section was stabilized with chalk blocks and turved over. Turves were removed when drier conditions necessitated deeper excavations and another tier was placed over the previous layer and then turved over again.*

There was no master plan to build Silbury Hill. It was designed and built according to prevailing circumstances at the time. Each terrace, each stage, each layer of the structure in turn representing a final and definite stand-alone phase. The evidence for this can clearly be established from the methods employed in constructing the initial central core right through to the uppermost terrace of Phase Three.

It has been suggested that each of the six terraces of the third construction phase may have been built up in triangular block sections and grassed over on the sides as work progressed to prevent erosion. But here again the individual terraces were not built in one continuous operation. Not only was there a significant pause between the construction of each terrace but also between the individual block sections of each terrace if indeed they were constructed in such a way *(Fig. 10)*.

Since there was no intent by the builders to enlarge the hill or increase its height any further, one may safely speculate that the top of each terrace was also grassed over. However, parts of this top layer of turves were removed again for each successive block-section of the next terrace when climatic conditions and a lower water table necessitated further excavations.

The trench surrounding part of the base of the hill was enlarged and deepened to tap into ground-water levels. The excavated material was deposited on top of the previous terrace, then stabilised by chalk blocks and grassed over once more. It seems likely that the storage basin to the west and north was also extended at the same time as the trench was dug deeper.

The removal of the turfed top layer prior to depositing more material for the next terrace would account for the complete absence of any insect remains, pollen, seeds and other organic material between the terraces. Even if the last section of various stages had not been grassed over after completion it would still have taken tens of years for even a thin organic layer to form and be visible as a dark horizon between the chalk deposits.

Whatever the circumstances, worm activity, chemical weathering and mixing within the hill would have destroyed any evidence there might have been to establish dates and some significant pauses between the construction of the various terraces of Phase Three and indeed also for the encapsulated first and second mounds of Phase One and Phase Two.

Tunnelling and the collapse of the old tunnels and penetration of present day molluscs, seeds and pollen into the excavated areas would have further accelerated the mixing process within the hill *(Fig. 26 & Fig. 27)*. Any attempt to provide precise dates for all three phases must therefore always be inconclusive.

Various accounts describe the gleaming, impressive pure whiteness of the finished chalk mound, which was no doubt a joy to behold when viewed from a distance. However, this may just be a romantic notion since each phase of the construction, with long intervals between, was immediately grassed over.

In any case, tucked away on the floor of a heavily wooded and at times very marshy vale and shrouded by trees higher up it cannot have been the intention of the Neolithic builders to construct the hill in a commanding position to be seen from afar.

Silbury Hill appears incomplete and unfinished. It seems as if the builders had lost interest in their project. The truncated 30 m wide flat top lacks the prominence, the aura of importance, the splendour and magnitude befitting such a structure – the hill was probably never meant to be a grand symbol of superior tribal authority or a visible territorial statement *(Fig. 11)*.

It was the change in climate to wetter conditions which resulted in the final, but apparently incomplete, appearance of the hill. The excavations had come to an end. There was again a plentiful supply of water throughout the year. The hill, merely a by-product of their gigantic efforts to reach and to store water, had served its purpose.

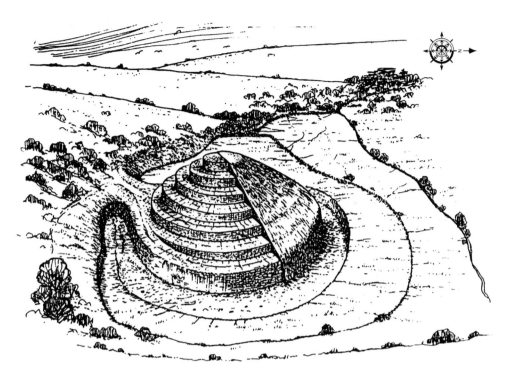

Fig.11   *The finished mound covered with turves and surrounded in parts by a trench of irregular*
width and depth broadening out to a water storage extension to the west. A single causeway
led across to higher ground.

One of the many detailed and bewildering calculations put forward over the years suggest
that it would have taken about 1,000 men 18 million hours over ten years to build Silbury
Hill. There is a confusing array of some very impressive statistics available in various
records. But do such statistics and calculations, the measurements and quantities involved
in this particular instance really matter? Perhaps not. They are of little meaning in the
final evaluation.

Silbury Hill was built in many stages over an extremely long period of time as and when
the need arose for a constant supply of water. In the absence of any precise dating one can
only guess at the probable duration. It may have been one hundred years, two hundred or
three hundred years. Whatever time frame there may have been, the most likely scenario
was that the building of other monuments on the nearby Downs and the lengthy
piece-meal construction of Silbury Hill were contemporaneous.

In addition to their other ongoing major projects and their daily hunting and farming
activities it was well within the capacity of the large settlements on the Downs to supply the
extra manpower urgently needed from time to time to deepen the trenches and in
consequence enlarge the hill. Life expectancy of the Neolithic people was only 35 to 40 years.
Every generation was forced to make the search for water their priority, irrespective of any
other projects in hand at that particular time.

Different generations also had different ideas of how to proceed and enlarge the mound with the excavated material when drier seasons threatened their water supply. Progress and change was inevitable. They had moved on and gained more experience in adapting to the ever-changing environment.

With the passage of time different building techniques evolved and were applied. They were quite distinct and are clearly reflected in the three main construction phases. Such increased knowledge and understanding of their immediate surroundings also resulted in a temporary water storage area surrounding part of the hill.

Quite unintentionally, the water storage area had become a lake *(Fig. 12)*. Over the years a certain amount of clay accumulated on the floor creating an impervious layer, thus allowing water to stay much longer above the water table during the now infrequent drier periods than the builders had experienced until then.

The clay, more precisely the 'Clay-with-Flints' as it is known, is a residual deposit from weathered chalk, a mixture of reddish clay with numerous unrolled flint nodules. This may have become mixed with the remnants of sands and clays which covered the chalk. Over millions of years erosion removed most of this material but substantial pockets still remain on the Chalk Downs and elsewhere from where the clay rich soil is washed down into coombes and vales.

Fig. 12   *View from the west. The rough outline of the lake, the water storage area which was created by Neolithic man, can be clearly seen. Note the faint indication of three terraces on the left, below the top of the hill. Also the spring water erosion feature in the right foreground.*

WHY A HILL?

The question may arise as to why was it necessary to build a hill if the excavated material could have been disposed of in some other way. Several decisive factors have to be considered to arrive at an answer.

The most important point overriding every other aspect is the fact that there was no intention by the Neolithic communities to build any hill at all. In the beginning they merely scooped out a shallow circular channel in the river gravels on the floor of the vale to reach the water table and collect and store whatever water there was available. The dug-out material was heaped up to form a small mound at the base of the chalk spur projecting down into the dried-up valley floor.

When the depth and size of their initial excavation proved insufficient to reach and hold water it was a natural progression, albeit with long intervals in between, that they would deepen the trench and in consequence increase the size and height of the initial and subsequent mounds. Under the circumstances this was the easiest and most effective option available once they had started constructing a mound.

Suitable space for the chalk debris in close proximity was extremely limited. The broad vales towards Avebury and Beckhampton and the extensive low ground leading towards Waden Hill and Swallowhead springs prevented adequate disposal of the excavated material. The only suitable sites available were on the wooded fringes of the low ground and on the elevated surroundings of the seasonal swampy vales.

With the passing of time, large amounts of chalk rock were also quarried from the chalk promontory on the southern side of the hill to locate the source of the Silbury springs. This was in addition to the large quantity of material from the water storage extensions adjacent to the deep trench which was now surrounding part of the hill. That material could only be efficiently disposed of by taking it across a natural, broad causeway, left in situ in the original chalk rock, to the top of the existing mound which was, not by intent or design, already half the height and size of the final structure.

The Neolithic builders would have known that freely deposited chalk or soil can only be heaped up to a limited height before it moves rapidly downhill again or be subjected to rapid erosion unless it was properly stabilised. They gained ample experience in these matters whilst digging the 18 m deep ditch surrounding the Avebury stone circles. Their emphasis was therefore on stabilisation. Lesser effort was required to dispose of the material on top of an already stabilized mound rather than utilize the surrounding higher ground some little distance away.

The builders also realized that it was not a viable proposition to leave the excavated material on the floor of the vales. In spite of the extreme seasonal dryness, the vales were at other times of the year waterlogged, very marshy and occupied by many streamlets. Any heaped-up material on the valley floor would have very quickly filled up the dug-out areas again. They had very few choices for adequate disposal. A mound built up by successive stages was the most practical and labour-efficient solution.

Although the frequency and duration of drier periods increased over many generations they did not extend throughout the year even though some years were drier than others. By the same token, some years were wetter, much wetter, than others without the need to dig for water.

Climate does not change in a day, in a week or in a month, but over many years, over tens or hundreds of years. The climate of the Sub-boreal period *(Fig. 29)* in Neolithic times, 5000 years ago was spasmodically warm with long periods of drought.

There can be no doubt that at various intervals many shallow troughs and trenches were dug on the valley floor to collect and store water, only to be filled in again by sediments during the wetter seasons, long before the permanent, well stabilized three mounds which make up Silbury Hill were constructed. This would account for the wide range of inconclusive radiocarbon dating obtained from the mixture of organic and other material apparently derived from several locations in the vicinity and found within the central core of the mound.

Due to the manner of construction, older material may also be present with younger material in the top layers of Silbury Hill, similar to the confusion existing in the bottom layers.

Three separate mounds were built. One on top of the other with long pauses in between. Each mound reflecting a different construction method. Every time a new mound was built over the previous one, the depth of the surrounding trench and adjacent area was made deeper and wider *(Fig. 13)*.

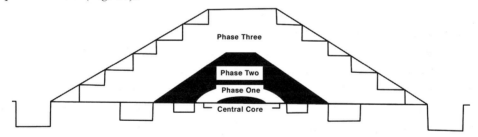

Fig. 13 *Cross section of Silbury Hill illustrating the Central Core followed by three separate construction phases and four progressively deeper trenches. (Not to scale.)*

There was a distinct purpose for their excavations. The mounds were constructed during long and completely dry periods in their desperate search for water. Whilst there was water there was no reason for digging trenches or enlarging any existing structure. It is utterly inconceivable that they would build three entirely self-contained mounds on top of each other, separated by extremely long intervals in a wooded, permanently swampy vale, standing chest-deep in mud and water *(Fig. 14)*. An undertaking in such circumstances would have been completely alien to Neolithic culture and tradition. As can be seen by the other structures on the Downs there were many more suitable locations on dry and elevated ground in the immediate vicinity to build a large hill for any other reason than securing an adequate water supply.

Fig. 14 *A present day equivalent of the conditions which may have existed in the marshy vale before Silbury Hill was built.*

The present is the key to the past, but so is simplicity. The obvious is too often overlooked in favour of some complicated explanation. There must have been some urgent and unusual circumstances to build a stabilised mound covering an inner wattle-fenced central core merely for it to be covered over by a second stabilised mound and for this to be followed by a third, still larger fully stabilised mound, covering both the original structures *(Fig. 13)*.

Necessity is the mother of all inventions. It was the changing climate and environment, the lack of water, which dictated all their actions as and when the need arose.

THE SPRINGS AND THE KENNET

The land around Silbury Hill is different today to that of 4500 to 5000 years ago. There have been subtle changes, albeit slight, but nevertheless important in relation to the total picture of the prehistoric period.

There was no definite course for the meandering multi-channelled Kennet. There was probably no river as such at all as we know today. Probably just small streams with varying amounts of water depending upon the seasons.

The valley was marshy and for parts of the year, a completely waterlogged area. This extended towards the West Overton flood-plain and also towards Beckhampton and well beyond Avebury where it then broadened out towards Berwick Bassett and Yatesbury. In consequence direct access to the Neolithic settlements on Windmill Hill from Avebury *(Fig. 4)* would have been much restricted during certain times of the year.

It was erosion over the past 5000 years and in part, human intervention, which finally carved out the course for the Kennet and accentuated and altered the valley contours shaped by permafrost conditions after the last Ice Age. Intensive farming, soil-creep and silting-up have also levelled many features in the surrounding area. As the vale deepened, more spring outlets appeared.

The Kennet was put into a straight jacket at the edge of the present field system when a causeway for the A4 Marlborough road was built near the base of the mound to straddle the frequently flooded vale. In consequence, the outflow channels of several springs were reversed or displaced in line with the new lay-out. This in turn altered the drainage system of the area and subsequent erosion pattern.

The original, diagonal course of the Kennet can still be clearly seen in the meadows to the east and south of Silbury Hill and near the Waden Hill springs. Parts of it are still flooded during wet periods.

However, interfering with nature does not always work. The very steep sides of the river in particular to the south of Silbury Hill are evidence of the rapid undercutting at the edge of the vale, in spite of the small tree plantation on top to prevent further erosion.

Some of the most important changes in the landscape were caused by running water, the very commodity so scarce at certain times during the Neolithic period. Five thousand years of spring sapping, the erosional process caused by water flowing from springs, have left their mark in the immediate surroundings.

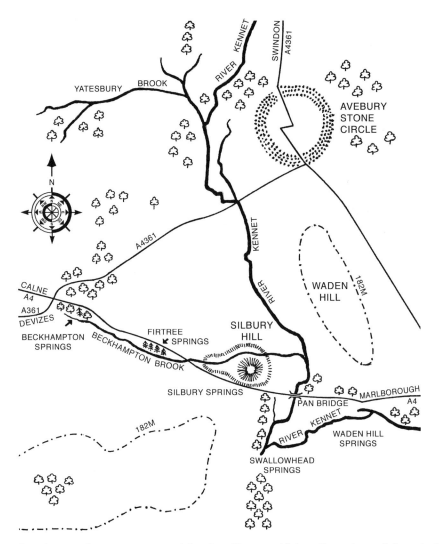

Fig. 15 *Plan showing drainage pattern of the river Kennet with its tributaries and the principal springs central to the construction of Silbury Hill.*

Numerous springs feeding into the Kennet today are the dominant feature in the vicinity of Silbury Hill. Only the Swallowhead springs are marked on the Ordnance Survey maps but there are many others and more prolific springs flowing from the chalk spurs into the vale which are not marked *(Fig. 15)*. They include the Waden Hill, the Silbury, the Firtree and Beckhampton springs; the last three named by the author for ease of reference.

The Waden Hill springs with their strong and steady flow have considerably steepened the narrow river passage to the east resulting in a near vertical escarpment. Even more pronounced have been the effects on the terrain by the Silbury springs on the southern side of the hill. These are the very springs Neolithic man tried to locate within the sloping chalk spur in their desperate search for water. Now they are gradually undercutting the foundations of the A4 Marlborough road in several places. The edge and slope of the pavement near the Silbury Hill viewpoint are slowly breaking away.

The Firtree springs, a little to the west and diagonal to the entrance of the Silbury Hill view point, are also migrating towards the A4 Marlborough road foundations but from the opposite side. However, a band of hard chalk within the chalk rock is limiting the erosional processes.

Water from the Firtree springs and the Beckhampton Brook, as well as from the Beckhampton springs further to the west is channelled through the narrow coombe, then across the former 'lake' and past Silbury Hill into the Kennet. In days gone by this too would have been an extremely marshy, waterlogged area stretching well beyond the present Beckhampton roundabout along the lower part of the A361 Devizes road.

The spring-lines giving rise to the Silbury, Firtree and Beckhampton springs are central to the construction of Silbury Hill. It may therefore seem strange that they attract such scant comment in explaining the reasons for the great mound.

The Swallowhead springs are probably one of the better known springs in the area today because they are marked on Ordnance Survey Maps. The location of the Swallowhead springs on old maps is actually shown further downstream where the present Waden Hill springs are; the latter are not shown. However it is now accepted that the Waden Hill springs are to the east of Silbury Hill adjacent to the A4 Marlborough road and the Swallowhead springs lie to the south, in a corner across a field leading up to the West Kennett Long Barrow.

Under normal climatic conditions, the Swallowhead springs are very seasonal with a relatively small outflow in comparison with the Waden Hill springs which are much more active, even during long, dry periods. They are also one of the last springs to dry up in the vicinity of Silbury Hill.

In spite of such variations, it is the Swallowhead springs which have been singled out and given a sacred status. They have become a connection to the spiritual world of the Neolithic people and visible tributes are still being paid to this day, leaving the important Waden Hill springs, Silbury Hill springs and other springs in the area rather neglected.

There is a possibility that the Swallowhead springs with their two outlets close together at right angles at the foot of a gentle sloping coombe did not even exist in Neolithic times. They were certainly not in their present position. Detailed research by the author has put them further north near the original course of the Kennet in the field bordering the A4 Marlborough road.

It would be a fallacy to simply assume that nothing has changed over 5000 years in the immediate vicinity of Silbury Hill. In consequence, it may seem rather surprising that the mysteries, legends and explanations, which have emerged over recent times, have all been based on the present landscape, on the present position of the many springs and on the present course of the river Kennet. This is greatly misleading and another vital flaw in some interpretations of the past, attempting to explain the meaning and purpose of the great mound and its surroundings.

THE CAUSEWAY AND SILBURY SPRINGS

Further evidence of spring sapping can be seen near the eroded remains of the once broad causeway which joins the hill to the chalk ridge, albeit in a much changed and more modest, form today. Much reduced in height and width by the past actions of the Silbury springs, the *'western causeway'* is now a mere shadow of its original size, flanked by large spring-head alcoves on either side.

At first glance this may appear to present quite a problem because the present topography on the southern side of the hill may suggest two walkways separated by a deep trench. However, under closer examination, there appears to be only one causeway leading from the crest of the chalk promontory across to the hill. Some old records also indicate only one broad access from the highest point of the chalk spur *(Fig. 16)*.

Although headward retreat of the spring-head alcove to the east of the causeway threatens to undercut the road foundations, the natural discharge is rather limited at present, even during prolonged and extremely wet periods.

Hazard posts on the edge of the pavement used to warn the unwary from venturing too close to the edge; the area is now secured by a fence.

Due to an altered drainage system and continuous extraction of groundwater, some of the water from the Silbury springs is now flowing in the opposite direction on the other side of the road, close to a metal-cased well head.

What appears to be a second causeway, referred to sometimes as the *'eastern causeway'*, is not an original feature. The present narrow ridge is merely the result of soil creep and artificial banking to prevent water from flowing into the hollow during frequent flooding of the area around Silbury Hill and thus causing further erosion. It also allowed access to the hill across the silted-up trench when groundwater levels were higher or during extremely wet periods.

The ridge, however, prevents adequate drainage of that particular closed-in area. The deep hollow adjacent to the western causeway is still slightly waterlogged at times, accelerating damage to the road foundations. It is mainly surface run-off from the road above, via a covered drain by the side of the pavement, supplemented at various intervals by spring water seepage and accumulated rain water on the silty clay floor.

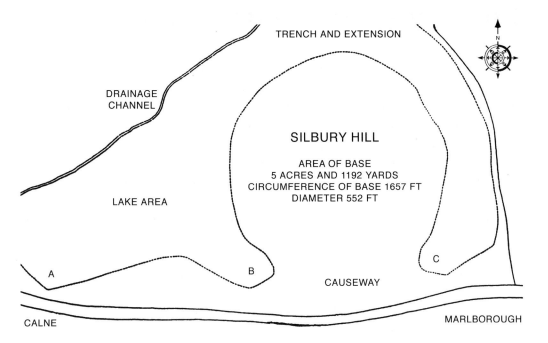

Fig. 16 *An 1862 ground plan of Silbury Hill shows only one broad causeway to the south. Worth noting is the irregular shaped base of the hill and spring erosion at points A,B and C. The present drainage channel for the Firtree and Beckhampton springs may not be an original feature.*

The high ground by the side of the road, just above the *'eastern causeway'* is not the original land surface, but heaped up material from building the modern road. The present raised ground does not follow the sloping contours of the chalk spur coming in from the south.

The ditch surrounding the hill was meant to collect and retain water and eventually drain into the excavated east and west extensions. Had there been an *'eastern causeway'* there would have been no drainage outlet for the abundant outflow from the Silbury spring adjacent to the main causeway. There was little point in digging a ditch in front of the most vigorous springs at that time to merely retain the outflow in a very restricted area between two walls of chalk rock, between two causeways. Access to such a narrow section of trench would have been very limited and completely unsuitable for any practical purpose. As mentioned elsewhere in the book the question of a moat for defence does not arise.

The causeway may have followed the original sloping ground contours or it may have been built up gradually to follow a horizontal line which would have allowed access to the higher parts of the hill, well beyond the halfway mark.

An elevated causeway would have certainly aided progress during construction of the middle and uppermost tiers of Silbury Hill. It is not clear which of these options was pursued by the Neolithic people, keeping in mind that the various stages of the hill represent a time span stretching over scores of generations. Some diagrams and sketches show a horizontal causeway, but this may be for illustration purposes only.

The deeper part of the Neolithic excavations at the base of Silbury Hill, the much acclaimed moat, was not really a feature in the true sense of the word. The width of the trench varied considerably and was more in the shape of a horseshoe which did not extend or encircle the south side of the hill. This side was in part occupied by the broad causeway and the relatively narrow drainage channel for the Silbury spring on the eastern side. The spring on the western side of the causeway drained directly into the 'lake' and ditch at the base of the hill. A partial excavation across the ditch on the south side appears to indicate that the outer edge of the ditch lies somewhere under the A4 Marlborough road. It is most unlikely that a modern road would have been built on the edge of such a steep slope with the additional danger of serious subsidence. There is no evidence of a stabilised road foundation on the sides of the south ditch.

The present hollows, spring-head alcoves, migrating south towards the edge of the pavement on either side of the sunken causeway are the result of comparatively recent erosion caused by spring sapping.

Approaching the hill from a westerly direction, the road climbs up the slope and veers slightly towards Silbury Hill, skirting very close to its base and then veers away again from the hill on its down slope in the direction of Marlborough. Had there been spring-head alcoves, the road would have followed a straight course across the chalk spur, completely bypassing the unwelcome obstruction. Even the original dirt track, the forerunner of the modern road, would have avoided such obstacle without the need for filling in. The old road could have easily taken a slightly southerly route further up the slope following the line of the Roman road.

SILBURY HILL – THE SHRINE

All the actions of the Neolithic people were invariably connected with their Gods or some mysterious powers they believed in, which directed their lives and made their existence possible. Having solved the problem of obtaining water and storing it for use throughout the year may have demanded a need for thanksgiving to the Great Goddess, the Mother of all Earth, or whatever else they worshiped.

Silbury Hill was not built as a shrine *(Fig. 17)*. However, over many generations it may have become a focal point, an icon of their lives and spiritual perspectives. Gradually, as work progressed in their successful search for water, the Hill possibly became an altar to pay tribute to the unseen and unknown forces of the Heaven, the World and the Universe.

The springs, providing life-giving water, so important in their struggle for existence, would have become a connection to the sacred world beneath their feet – a passage to the mythical centre of the Earth. They were a link to the womb of the Great Goddess, the navel of the world.

In the passage of time the Neolithic communities may have also seen Silbury Hill as a Harvest Hill associated with summer, the ripening and harvesting of crops. The Hill represented a monumental image of the Silbury Mother Goddess, the Great Provider in their lives.

Fig. 17 *Silbury Hill from the south-east. There it stands, secluded and completely detached from the other prehistoric structures in appearance and location. The flat, truncated, slightly oval top may have become an ideal setting for the Neolithic people to pay tribute to the unseen forces which regulated their lives – a means for the celebration of life and death.*

Throughout the following centuries the meaning and purpose of Silbury Hill standing forlorn in a hollow on the Downs had spawned an ever-increasing aura of mystery and colourful ideas. The Hill evolved in modern times as a symbol of various beliefs and customs which differ as much as the many explanations of its existence.

THE MARLBOROUGH MOUNT

The Marlborough Mount in the grounds of Marlborough College 9 km to the east along the Kennet valley may have some affinity with Silbury Hill *(Fig. 18)*. Both are situated on waterlogged, swampy ground, in a hollow by a river, near some very active springs and both within easy reach of large Neolithic settlements on the surrounding Downs.

The steep-sided chalk mound, 18 m in height, 83 m in diameter at the base and 31 m across the top, is approximately half the size of Silbury Hill.

Fig. 18 *The wooded Marlborough Mount in the grounds of Marlborough College. Note the Sarsen stone wall in the foreground, the Grotto with curved archway built into the mound, lower right of picture and the spiral walkway to the top between the trees.*

Landscaping over the centuries and a boiler house, complete with chimney, at the very base as well as a grotto cut into the southern side, have transformed the external appearance of the mound. A spiral walkway, probably not an original feature, leads to the heavily wooded top. Various garden features and access roads to school buildings have totally obliterated any remains of a trench or other excavations that might have surrounded the mound. The steep sides, having withstood the ravages of time, point to a layered, well-stabilized construction utilising chalk blocks, flints and Sarsen stones.

There is the distinct possibility that this mound was also built in several stages starting with just a small initial mound, a central core, from a scooped out area on the dried-out valley floor. This may have been succeeded by a larger mound as the climate changed to drier conditions, then finally by a tiered arrangement similar to Silbury Hill. Some of the adjacent low ground may also have formed part of the unique water storage and collecting sites during Neolithic times.

A huge catchment area on the surrounding chalklands drains directly onto the lower ground around the Marlborough Mount. An extensive Clay with Flints cover to the south allows surface water to collect into streams rather than disappearing into the permeable chalk rock. In consequence, some water was probably available for much longer in comparison with the conditions at Silbury Hill when the climate finally changed to long and extremely dry phases in the Sub-boreal period.

The top of the water table in Neolithic times was also much closer to the ground surface here than at Silbury Hill. This would have meant shallower excavations in their search for water and in effect a smaller mound. The same difference in groundwater levels between Silbury Hill and the Marlborough Mount still exist today irrespective of the continuous extraction by the water authorities. Although the chalklands and certain features may have changed quite considerably over the past 5000 years, the internal structure of the chalk determining the position of the water table, will have remained fairly stable over such a relatively short period.

Little is known about the age, purpose and the various construction phases of the Marlborough Mount. No detailed research or radiocarbon dating has been carried out to provide some clues for its existence. Any observations and comparisons with Silbury Hill must therefore be rather speculative, even though striking similarities do exist which cannot be simply ignored or dismissed. The circumstantial evidence is rather compelling. Taking the topography and the unusual location into consideration, the construction of the Marlborough Mount and Silbury Hill may be contemporaneous, even though there may be subtle differences.

THE HATFIELD BARROW AND MARDEN HENGE

Monumental mounds of the Neolithic period like Silbury Hill and Marlborough Mount, are of exceptional rarity. A further example, not far south of the Marlborough Downs, is the Hatfield Barrow within the Marden Henge, near the village of Marden in the Vale of Pewsey *(Fig. 19)*.

It was a comparatively low, domed feature, approximately 70 m in diameter and over 9 m high. Surrounding the structure was a ditch 28 m wide and 105 m in external diameter. The depth of the ditch is not known.

Excavations showed no signs of burial nor did they yield any evidence which may have determined the purpose of the mound. The work caused a collapse of the unstable centre and as a result the barrow was levelled in 1818.

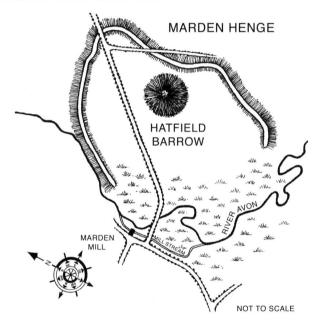

Fig. 19 *Marden Henge and Hatfield Barrow in the Vale of Pewsey.*

The underlying geology of the Pewsey Vale is quite different to that of the Chalk Downs. The topography is dominated by Greensand and underlying Gault Clay, which are slightly older rocks, below the Chalk formations.

In consequence, the Hatfield Barrow, also referred to as the Hatfield Mound, was not built from chalk but from local rock, the Greensand, and probably stabilized by rocks from hard layers within the Greensand formation.

Some of the surface features in the Pewsey Vale are also covered by drift deposits of chalky gravels and a loamy brown clay swept into the vale during the last Ice Age.

The Marden Henge is an irregularly formed enclosure covering about 35 acres and surrounded by a ditch of equally irregular dimensions. It was built in the shape of a horseshoe on slightly elevated ground in a sweeping bend of the present-day Salisbury Avon. The open side of the enclosure was bounded by the edge of the River Avon floodplain. Sited near the eastern entrance and within the Henge was the Hatfield Barrow.

Built about 2900 BC to 2400 BC in the late Neolithic period, the monument fits into the same broad time frame as Silbury Hill and Marlborough Mount. The latter of course with some reservations. Again there is some inconsistency in the various records relating to the dates and size, not only of the Marden Henge, but also of the Hatfield Barrow within the enclosure – a factor which is common to other monuments of the Neolithic/Bronze age era on the Downs and immediate surroundings.

The Hatfield Barrow, in spite of its comparatively modest size and unique location within an enclosure, shares nevertheless striking similarities with Silbury Hill and Marlborough Mount.

There is the extremely permeable rock structure here – not chalk, but greensand – the unique disposal of the excavated material forming a mound – the unusually, low location of the henge – the marshy and at times completely waterlogged ground nearby – the undulating elevations in close proximity which were not exploited – the absence of an established river system – the many meandering streamlets near their settlements shifting their course from season to season – the unlimited supply of water in a stable climatic environment – the lack of Neolithic artifacts and finally, despite its name, the Hatfield Barrow was not a burial mound.

The comparison with Silbury Hill and Marlborough Mount on the Chalk Downs could not be more appropriate.

In consequence, the gradual climate change to prolonged drier conditions and the drying up of springs and infant streams would have had the same dire effect on the land and its people, on the edge of the normally marshy Greensand vale, as much as it affected the settlements on the nearby Chalk Downs.

The only means of obtaining water for the large settlements in and around the henge entailed excavating down to the water table to find the source of the springs. This is of course on the assumption that the henge, larger than Avebury, served not only as a ceremonial feature but also as a permanent shelter for the Neolithic people.

It is not known if the Hatfield Mound was built in several stages as levelling of the structure has unfortunately destroyed all evidence there may have been.

However, it would not be entirely out of place to assume that increasingly longer periods of dryness might have necessitated several construction phases applying different techniques as successive generations excavated ever deeper to locate the frequently disappearing water table.

Greensand is often soft and unstable. This accounts for the relatively shallow domed construction and rather extensive width of the surrounding trench. The deeper the trench to reach groundwater levels, the greater the width at the top of the trench.

Only a few sections of Marden Henge remain to this day. Natural erosion and farming has obliterated most of its defining features and more than just a modest amount of imagination is now required to visualise the sheer size of this ancient monument.

THE WEST KENNETT PALISADE ENCLOSURES

One of the lesser known Neolithic sites in the vicinity of Avebury is that of the West Kennett Palisade Enclosures situated in an approximate alignment 1 km east of Silbury Hill and some 800 m west of the Sanctuary *(Fig. 20)*.

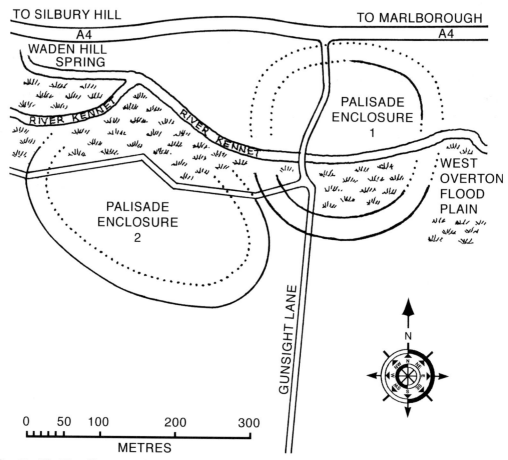

Fig. 20 *The West Kennett Palisade Enclosures east of Silbury Hill.*

Though there is no precise dating, it seems reasonable to place its construction between 2900 BC and 2100 BC. This puts the West Kennett Palisade Enclosures into the same time frame as Silbury Hill, albeit with perhaps shorter construction periods.

Only a few sections of two palisade enclosures have been located. One site is to the south of the Kennet, and close by, slightly diagonal to the north-east of the river, lies the site of the other enclosure. Both sites were hemmed in between opposite slopes of the surrounding chalk hills and both occupied some of the low marshy ground of the vale with the latter actually straddling the present course of the Kennet.

There may not have been an active river at the time of the palisade enclosures, even though the narrow vale was the only drainage outlet for the numerous streamlets and springs from an area stretching well beyond Avebury and Winterbourne Bassett to the North, as well as Beckhampton and Yatesbury to the West *(Fig. 4 & Fig. 15)*.

The location of the West Kennett Palisade Enclosures within and on the fringe of a marshy vale is therefore most surprising and does not fit easily into the general pattern of Neolithic settlements on the Chalk Downs.

It must be assumed that construction of the enclosures was overtaken by climatic events well beyond the control of the builders in the same way as the activities around Silbury Hill were entirely controlled by similar vagaries of climate, but of course for different reasons.

It is not known if both enclosures were built at the same time or even if they were ever completed on account of their most unlikely location. The horseshoe configuration points to incomplete structures and it is not known how long they existed or how large the communities were within these two settlements. However, one may speculate that they were certainly involved in the desperate search for water and the consequent lengthy and deep excavations resulting in the building of Silbury Hill.

As the climate changed, the vale turned gradually into a permanent swamp and marsh land once again and no doubt the waterlogged enclosures faced abandonment, except perhaps for some parts on enclosed higher ground. Climate may have favoured settlement at that particular location when the narrow vale was comparatively dry but climate change may have also eventually destroyed their very existence. Today however there is very little visible evidence on the ground of those rather unusual prehistoric structures.

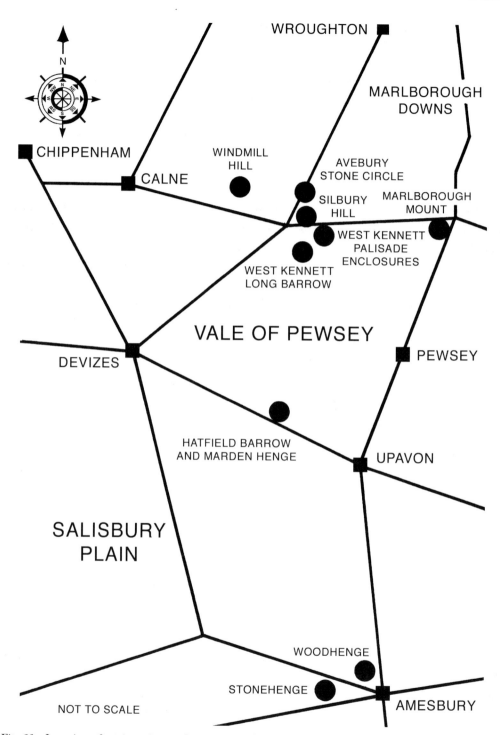

Fig. 21 *Location of ancient sites and monuments featured in text. There is no apparent correlation between the various sites, their position being entirely determined by the natural environment.*

THE ROMANS AT SILBURY HILL

During the Roman occupation, approximately 2000 years ago, a Roman road was built which followed a course directly above Silbury Hill to the south and dipped down across the river Kennet at the narrowest point of the vale and up again to Waden Hill on the other side.

The Romans may have constructed a bridge at that point or they may have simply forded the river and the narrow, swampy vale. Further downstream the frequently flooded Kennet Vale and water meadows broadened out significantly making crossing very difficult, perhaps even impossible at certain times of the year due to flooding.

The availability of water at the foot of Silbury Hill made it an ideal place for Roman troops to establish a permanent staging post where they could camp, rest and refresh themselves in the multitude of springs emerging from the base of the chalky slopes.

To them, Silbury Hill and its many springs had no special ceremonial or religious significance. The hill and the springs just happened to be there. As a matter of fact they were probably more of an inconvenience because the Roman road had to skirt around the hill and the marshy areas, creating a troublesome diversion in their road alignment. Nevertheless, they may have wondered why such an unusual feature adorned the local landscape, straddling the course of their intended road. There is also evidence of several Roman settlements near the hill.

However, intermittent climate change showed itself again during parts of the Roman occupation when drier seasons in some years were once again much in evidence. To overcome the periodic shortage of water during their occupation several wells were dug down to the lowest level of the water table when conditions demanded *(Fig. 22)*.

Four wells have been excavated and examined but there is evidence of a further two. After 2500 years wells had taken the place of large open water storage areas. Mankind had moved on. Two of the wells were actually used as disposal pits for kitchen waste and other domestic rubbish. This points to long intervals between the use of wells during extremely dry periods and subsequent longer periods of sufficient rainfall when the flow from the springs was again fully utilised rendering the wells superfluous.

One well was actually located in the middle of the main causeway leading to Silbury Hill and was still in use during the 18th century. In the absence of any Roman finds it may be modern. Severe erosion of the main causeway may, in part, be due to the existence of that particular well.

Another probable site of a Roman well may be the metal boxed well-head slightly east of Silbury Hill, on the opposite side of the road, or it may have been located immediately adjacent to it. The well was opened and examined in 1896. Various finds indicate it was in use from Roman times until the Middle Ages. A light patch of earth, visible after ploughing in the field to the south, directly above Silbury Hill, marks the site of another Roman well.

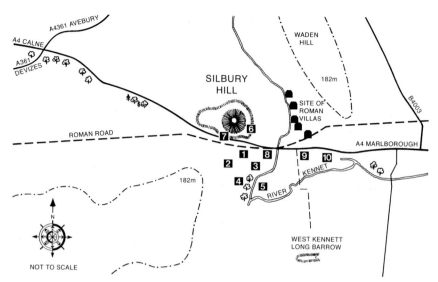

Fig. 22   *The Roman Road, wells and buildings in the immediate vicinity of Silbury Hill.*

1 & 2   Roman wells opened and examined in 1882 and 1896.
3 & 4   Roman wells filled with kitchen refuse and other Roman debris.
5 & 6   Roman wells unexamined.
7   Well in use during 18th century and situated in middle of causeway.
8   Site of present metal cased well head.
9 & 10   Wells in use until 19th century.

The Romans had to dig wells in response to long dry periods. The need for digging wells does not arise when there is an abundance of clear water, bubbling out from the many springs. Wells would have been dug as water levels fell below the springline in the chalk aquifers. This was a natural lowering of the water table. The climate was changing once again.

History had repeated itself.

The wells, between 7 m and 8 m deep, were all dug in the high ground not in the dry and lower ground of the vale where silting up and flooding during subsequent wetter seasons would have created immense difficulties. One Roman well, however, was found on the east side, at the foot of Silbury Hill, which is normally flooded during wet periods. Situated on the floor of the former wide trench area meant a less deep well was necessary to reach the water table. It was probably dug in a hurry to reach groundwater levels without giving much thought to the consequences of subsequent wetter seasons – further evidence of an extremely long period with dry conditions when the search for water became a dire necessity.

The Romans experienced the same problems as the Neolithic communities before them but due to their advanced technical knowledge were able to solve them in a different way.

Now, 2000 years on from Roman times, mankind has again turned to the chalklands for a supply of water. This time not by digging wells or trenches and building hills from the excavated materials but by extracting water directly from the chalk aquifers before it reaches open ground.

SILBURY HILL AND NEOLITHIC SOCIETY

Although history has put the Neolithic people on a pedestal, they were certainly not blessed with some superhuman mystical powers, nor did they possess extraordinary abilities way ahead of their time. They simply made use of the many opportunities around them and what the Earth could provide relative to their needs and beliefs.

On the one hand, we bestow some superior skills and advanced knowledge upon Neolithic people and on the other hand, we suggest a waterlogged burial mound in the middle of a swamp – a defensive position with nothing to defend – a gleaming white beacon as a symbol of power and influence to be seen from afar and a high visibility display making a strong territorial statement. But in spite of all these attributes the turf-covered hill was tucked away in the bottom of a normally marshy hollow surrounded by dense woodland.

They were not ahead of their time, even though there were some with a far-reaching vision and a distinct sense of purpose. Throughout history there have always been those who stood out above the rest, but like ourselves today, Neolithic people were on a perpetual learning curve.

Where they constructed unique monuments, stone circles and deep trenches, so present mankind built the Channel Tunnel, huge skyscrapers and sent rockets to the Moon. Everything is relevant within the time-frame of mankind's existence.

Nothing in nature is constant. Time has taken its toll. The aging Silbury Hill, the fabric now slowly crumbling away, stands today in a much-changed landscape which is in stark contrast to that in which ancient man walked some 5000 years ago.

There is some doubt as to whether the distinct stepped profile of the uppermost terraces is indeed an original feature or whether it has been modified at some later stage during medieval or earlier times. The reason for such modification, if indeed there were any, is unclear since the upper terraces continue the stepped contour of the outer part of the hill *(Fig. 23)*.

Recent observations also suggest that the hill may have been built in a spiral fashion. However, significant soil creep on the eastern side of the hill, especially near the top, has distorted not only the terraced construction, but has also caused that side to flatten out considerably, deforming the symmetry of the hill. There is also a distinct bulge halfway up the slope on that particular side. Slight downward movement has been further exacerbated by spring erosion near the base of the mound. This may have led to the spiral construction theory. The Silbury springs along the foot of the chalk promontory are still active during prolonged wet periods.

Fig. 23   *Silbury Hill from the east. Soil creep has exposed two of the stepped upper terraces and distorted the even symmetry of the hill. Spring sapping and undercutting is rapidly destroying the ancient structure.*

In the swirling mists of dark summer nights the ghosts of the distant past are still dancing on the water meadows around Silbury Hill. The legends live on. Reality and mystery appear to have blended smoothly into one with the romance and magic of the upper chalklands. Silbury Hill is many things to many people. The intention by the ancient people was not to build three hills on top of each other but to tap permanently into the seasonal water table levels as and when the need arose. Had there been no climate change Silbury Hill would not have been built. But in the final analysis, the Silbury Hill saga is a fitting tribute to the skilful exploitation of the local geology by Neolithic communities on the Downs in their desperate quest for water. Silbury Hill should really stand as a monument to the ingenuity of the Neolithic people to adjust to an ever-changing environment.

APPENDIX

SARSEN STONES

Throughout history mankind has always made use of the materials close to hand – Neolithic communities on the Downs were no exception. They made good use of that what the earth could provide. In due course the local geology was surprisingly well exploited and completely dictated their way of life.

Sarsen stones are central to the construction of many prehistoric monuments on the Chalk Downs and the dense accumulations of these stones within the vicinity were fully utilised. Numerous structures and monuments on the chalklands including Avebury and Stonehenge are visible evidence of their exploitation and adaptation to the natural environment. Because the Sarsen stones were there, and apparently alien to a chalkland environment, they may have became a symbol of Neolithic beliefs, culture and tradition on the Avebury Downs. The origin of the name Sarsen may have its roots in the Anglo-Saxon words 'sar' which stands for troublesome and 'stan' which means stone. Down the corridors of time the stones have also been known as bridestones or druidstones, but most commonly as grey wethers from their likeness to resting sheep which were known by the same name. From a distance with the sun disappearing over the horizon, a flock of sheep can easily blend in with scattered Sarsen stones in the undulating landscape of the upper chalklands.

There is however a much favoured version which suggests that 'Sarsen' is derived from the word 'Saracen' which means outlandish, a stranger, an alien. Both descriptions could in part be right, for a Sarsen is indeed an outlandish, troublesome stranger alien to the present environment. No doubt countless plough shares, broken by the hard blocks still lying under the surface, bear witness to such an apt description.

Over the centuries these stones across the Downs and elsewhere in southern England have inspired a sense of mystery, wonder and curiosity. Their origin and location has in the past been linked to magical powers, extraterrestrial events, volcanic activity and to forces within the earth not fully understood.

Although some doubts remain, it is now widely accepted that the Sarsens are of Early Tertiary age – of the Eocene era. The Eocene describes a period in the Earth's history some 50 million years ago.

Geological processes in those far off times gradually covered the underlying chalk formations of the earlier Cretaceous period with mud, sands and gravels. All were neatly deposited, one on top of the other, like layers in a chocolate cake, with occasional local variations in between. Sea levels and the climate changed. Sub-tropical temperatures in the Eocene gave rise to large tracts of desert. It was an environment where evaporation, in spite of seasonal high rainfall, exceeded precipitation.

In consequence sands and gravels were gradually cemented together beneath the flat desert surface by migrating siliceous and sometimes iron rich solutions. These minerals had slowly leached out from the bedrock due to groundwater rising from deep below by capillary action and were re-deposited to form a hard impervious surface layer known as a *'duricrust'*.

Cementation of sands and gravels was not uniform or was the depth of the hard crust. Intermittent periods of induration (the process by which sediments are hardened) produced layers of different colour, hardness and density. The finer sands when cemented formed an extremely tough rock, a hard quartzitic sandstone, and the larger pebbly beds formed a conglomerate of rounded, mostly water-worn pebbles.

During this period palm trees grew on the flat desert surface, their roots reaching deep into the sand to obtain moisture. The process of silicification also penetrated into the roots and, depending on time and depth, some parts of the root system were completely replaced by silica similar to the process which gave rise to the agatised trees in the Petrified Forest of Arizona, USA. The unsilicified root fragments decayed during the passage of time, leaving a series of cavities and tubes in the hard sandstone matrix that ranged in size.

Some sections of indurated layers of sandstone were deeply buried whilst others were uplifted and broken up by further geological processes. Subsequent weathering and erosion removed the less cemented portions, leaving the more resistant masses behind as the Sarsen stones. Freed from the twilight of the past by constant erosion of the surrounding land the Sarsens can now be found in dense accumulations scattered across various parts of the Downs and elsewhere in south-east England.

The process of induration can be observed at the present time in Australia and Africa where duricrusts develop over long periods, probably half a million years or more, on flat land surfaces which have remained comparatively free from erosion and tectonic upheaval.

Sarsens are large irregular blocks of a very hard sandstone, akin to quartzite, displaying marked lithological variations. Although they have originated at different times and under different conditions the presence of a siliceous cement remains a distinguishing feature of all Sarsens. They are devoid of fossils except for the few silicified remnants of root fragments; strong evidence of a land-based environment.

The stones are composed of angular and sub-angular grains of coarse and fine quartz sand within the range of 0.5 – 0.05 mm. They are firmly cemented by secondary silica into an extremely durable, tough and abrasive rock of sugary appearance, with individual quartz grains glinting in strong sunlight.

Fig. 24   *Accumulation of Sarsen stones on the Marlborough Downs.*

There are few bedding planes and joints although faint indication of cross bedding may be observed in some stones. The colour varies from grey through to yellow and white, but the white Sarsens are much softer and weather more readily.

Some stones grade progressively from a fine grained to a coarse grained texture across distinct sedimentation planes. Few may consist of cemented silt or loam. Others show single or small patches of flint inclusions or are a conglomerate with closely packed rounded or sub-angular flints, known as the '*Hertfordshire Puddingstones*'.

The surfaces of a large number of Sarsen stones, both on the Marlborough Downs and elsewhere, show patches of ferruginous staining – a brownish film of weathered iron minerals. On some stones a hard layer of haematite (iron oxide) has formed, similar to desert varnish which, when weathered, displays a grey to reddish-brown texture.

The ravages of time have produced Sarsens of varying shapes. The softer, less resistant material has eroded leaving on one side an uneven surface with deep channels, troughs, depressions, rounded knobs and lumps. The opposite side is frequently pierced by straight, tapering and stepped root tubes of varying sizes penetrating deep into the stone and sometimes emerging on the other side. These unusual features can best be seen on upright Sarsens much to the puzzling wonderment of many a visitor to the Avebury stones.

Some root holes are slightly iron stained on the inside whilst others display a halo of light coloured sand grains at the outer edges. Weathering has exposed fragments of silicified roots in tubes and holes. Further erosion has produced open channels with remnants of agatised root material.

Many of the larger Sarsens are tabular with very few inclusions and irregularities. Induration has been consistent and complete resulting in an extremely hard rock. This is shown by distinct smooth and rounded surface weathering, so much a feature of granites and similar rock formations.

Frost-shattering along joints and planes of weakness has removed flat sections giving some stones a stepped profile and, in the case of standing stones, a top heavy appearance. Shallow dish-shaped hollows and pitting are another feature of these tabular, massive and dense-textured Sarsen stones.

In terms of size, height, weight and bulk the Sarsen stones show much variation and many configurations. A typical Sarsen is a very heavy and dense stone ranging from small irregular shaped boulders less than 50 cm across to several large blocks and megaliths several metres in diameter about 7 m in length, weighing up to 70 tons.

The Marlborough Downs form a block of about 50 square kilometres of chalkland intersected by many dry valleys strewn with Sarsens. A current estimate puts the number of these stones in the area at 25,000 with many more still lying buried (*Fig. 24*).

The unusual proliferation of these grey stones in the chalk landscape did not escape the attention of the Neolithic people some 5000 years ago. An aura of mystery and unseen forces surrounding the Sarsens in their strange settings took on a deep, religious meaning for them.

Evidence of their beliefs and the influence of the stones on their lives is shown in the megaliths of Avebury, West Kennett Avenue, Stonehenge and in their many burial sites on the chalklands. The Sarsen stones, supplemented with hard chalk rock, were also used within Silbury Hill to stabilize the mounds of Phase One and Phase Two.

The durable, abrasive nature of the Sarsens has also been utilised by the early settlers for sharpening and polishing cutting tools. Some stones are known by the french name of *'Polissoir'* (polisher). One such well-preserved example from the Neolithic era can be seen on Totterdown behind Delling Copse, and another on one of the standing stones which is situated at a point where the West Kennett Avenue traverses the road.

'Polissoirs' have several grooves for sharpening the cutting edges of tools and smooth surfaced, dish shaped hollows for polishing the faces of flint and stone axes. The 'Polissoir' in the West Kennett Avenue displays a coarse grained texture for sharpening, and a tough fine-grained texture for polishing, both on the same stone.

Several stones on the Downs display deep grooves on their dense and even textured surface. Some are perfectly parallel to each other whilst others have a random arrangement of grooves criss-crossing the stone. At first glance, and in the absence of any dish shaped hollows such features may appear to be glacial striation marks – grooves produced by rocks frozen into the base of a glacier. However, closer inspection shows them to be sharpening grooves similar to those found on the *'Polissoirs'*.

The chalk itself is devoid of good building stone except for a narrow band of hard chalk stone known as *'clunch'*. It is therefore of little surprise that Sarsens should have been used extensively throughout history as grinding stones for corn and as local building material.

Sarsens were also used in the repair of Windsor Castle and for setts to pave the Swindon tramways in place of granite.

Thousands upon thousands of Sarsen stones have been broken up and removed from the Downs since Neolithic times and many more have been moved to new locations by ancient and modern farmers to gain more land for cultivation. The present accumulation of Sarsens, plentiful though they appear to be, are but mere fragments of the former stone blanket which covered the Downs.

Generations of the Free and Cartwright families were the foremost stone masons on the Downs in recent times – the area is still littered with the evidence of their work. Angular blocks, split and marked stones, broken iron wedges, shattered fragments and pits, which were once occupied by the now removed Sarsens, are a stark reminder of their activities.

In due course modern materials replaced the Sarsens as building stones when it was discovered that cement mortar will not adhere to the stones. Only lime mortar can be used. Examples can be seen in the Avebury Stone Circles, West Kennett Avenue and in Piggledean Bottom where attempts have been made to reassemble some broken Sarsens with cement. This proved unsuccessful and brass and steel rods were used instead.

The stonemasons have now departed. Life has moved on and nature has reclaimed the disturbed and tortured land. Calm has returned.

We may know much of how the Sarsen stones were formed and what moved them to their present resting place. However, this has not diminished the aura of mystery and romance which surrounds the recumbent, brooding stones in the oasis of peace on the Marlborough Downs where time stood still.

CHALK AND FLINTS

Chalk determined the shape, simplicity and outstanding scenery in a large part of England. The rolling, undulating hills and deep coombes of the chalklands rising some 300 m above the surrounding countryside influenced the life and activities of Neolithic Man on the Downs.

Unlike the Sarsen stones which were hard, unyielding and difficult to handle the underlying chalk formations and large pockets of flinty clay with weathered chalk rock proved a relative easy material to work with, but most important of all, the chalk formations also yielded an abundance of large good quality flints for their tools and weapons.

Why a soft rock like chalk can form hills and maintain a relative height over thousands of years defying rapid weathering may at first glance appear a mystery. The answer is found in the porosity of the rock. Rainfall sinks quickly through the various layers leaving insufficient run-off on the surface to cause and accelerate erosion.

What is the special nature of the rock that can shape these gentle hills with their steep escarpments? What really is chalk? Where did it come from? A brief journey some 90 million years back in time to the late Cretaceous period will yield many clues as to its origin.

Situated south of its present position the area which was to form the British Isles was covered by an ancient sea. It was an age of apparent great activity giving rise to the landscape we know today, even though other parts in the life of our Planet were just as vibrant and momentous throughout time.

During the late Cretaceous period the advance of the ancient sea which blanketed a large part of future-Britain had reached its climax. The warm waters were teeming with a most prolific type of planktonic marine algae called coccospheres. When the algae died their remains, consisting of microscopic crystalline calcite scales, called coccoliths, sank to the sea floor and formed a white sediment which in time was to become chalk.

Recent research and the availability of powerful electron microscopes have indicated that algae may have been the staple food of shrimp-like creatures, called copepods. It is thought that for the scales, the coccoliths, to sink to the ocean floor they had to be first consumed and passed through the copepods. In consequence the specks of digested and then excreted food eventually built up a dense white ooze on the sea floor. Millions of years later this had solidified into chalk which was eventually uplifted to form land.

The size of the individual components in the chalk, as well as the time scale involved, are truly impressive. Most of the particles, fossils in their own right, are less than one thousandth of a millimetre in size and require above a x5000 magnification to be visible.

Furthermore, the build up rate of chalk was extremely slow. A mere 25 – 30 m in a million years. A time frame of such magnitude equates to a nearly negligible sedimentation rate of only one centimetre in 500 – 800 years or just one millimetre in 50 – 80 years. On the human scale of things this is nearly a non-event. Even fingernails and hair grows faster and the 'dance' of the continents around the globe, due to plate tectonic activity, seems to be rapid in comparison with the deposition of chalk.

Fig. 25 *A small chalk quarry in the Vale of Pewsey.*

In addition to the planktonic marine algae, larger fossils like the sea urchins, brachiopods, bivalves and belemnites are widespread throughout the chalk. The lower levels of the chalk also have some sponges and ammonites and the higher levels contain some sea lillies, or crinoids, as they are better known.

Chalk is an unadulterated limestone. It is nearly 98% pure calcium carbonate. When in contact with a weak acid it 'fizzes', giving off bubbles of carbon dioxide. It is soft, permeable, extremely fine grained and whitish to greyish in colour *(Fig. 25)*.

The brilliant whiteness of chalk is a result of its most unusual purity and the very small particles which increases the rock's reflectivity. It could be said that the extraordinary brightness of chalk is due to the captured sunshine of those far away days being eternally locked into the white ooze on the ocean floor!

Within the great depth of chalk deposits are several bands of impermeable clay and marl of varying thicknesses and also hard bands, such as the Melbourn Rock, used sometimes as building stone. The Melbourn Rock was named after the small village on the chalk in Cambridgeshire.

Flints are an integral part of the upper levels of the Chalk. There is a scarcity of flints in lower levels but their presence increases dramatically through the middle and into the uppermost part. They are extremely tough and inert and survive the weathering and erosion of the host rock. In spite of their hardness, they splinter easily displaying a conchoidal fracture and razor sharp edges when struck with a hammer.

Flints are formed from pure silica (98% silicon dioxide) and are basically quartz with a micro-crystalline or crypto-crystalline structure. They are found as irregularly shaped nodules, or sometimes as extremely weird and fanciful configurations, within the chalk formations.

When broken open, flints display a brown, glassy colour inside but the outer surface is pale grey or porcelain white, sometimes referred to as patina. The difference in colour is due to the escape of water which had filled the tiny voids between the crystals leaving microscopic air spaces on the outside with different light-reflecting properties, resulting in white or grey. Some broken pieces of flint may weather to a delicate shade of blue after lengthy exposure to the elements.

Chemically, flints are quite different from the calcium carbonate of chalk and many theories abound as to their origin. Nevertheless, it is generally accepted that the silica was derived from the siliceous skeletons of micro fossils, plankton and also from sponges that grew on the sea floor. The silica was subsequently dissolved in the warm waters of the sea and dispersed within the soft chalk sediments on the bottom of the Cretaceous ocean. Eventually the silica came out of solution and re-crystallised within the stabilized chalk deposits around areas of organic concentrations to form flints. Thus the sedimentation of chalk and the formation of flints were two separate events.

Flint is the forerunner of modern technology. Not only did it provide the spark to make fire but when prehistoric man discovered the art of flaking and chipping (knapping) it was used to make almost all his sharp-edged tools and weapons. As a matter of fact, for the greater part of human history tools and weapons consisted not of steel or iron, not of bronze or copper, but of flint.

The waters in the ancient oceans contained a small percentage of iron and sulphur which combined within the chalk sediments to form iron pyrites, better known as 'fool's gold'. Rusty-looking nodules containing blade-like, sharp pointed crystals radiating from a central core can be found, Pyrite also occurs as minute crystals scattered throughout the chalk. Weathered-out pyrite nodules are sometimes found on the surface of the chalk or even on beaches. Locally they have acquired the name of 'thunderbolts' and their formation and location has spawned some fanciful ideas; their presence being associated with UFOs and Aliens.

Mystery and magic are only part of the unique chalkland scenery. It has also shaped the destiny and the environment of Neolithic communities living and toiling on the Chalk Downs and influenced the construction of many monuments in the surrounding area. Silbury Hill is but one example.

Nature had served the Neolithic people extremely well.

HISTORY AND EXPLORATION OF SILBURY HILL

11TH CENTURY.

Silbury Hill was used as a Saxon fort.

1281

The mound was first recorded as *Seleburgh* and later in the 16th century as *Selbarrowe Hill*. The origin and meaning of those words as well as the present name of Silbury being rather uncertain. Many theories abound to explain its origin.

1663

Charles II visited the top of Silbury Hill.

1723

Tree planting recorded on top of the mound in the course of which a human burial was found. However, the remains were not of the Neolithic period.

1743

A detailed and illustrated account of the Hill was given by William Stukely.

1776/7

The Duke of Northumberland Shaft. A vertical shaft was sunk from the top of the mound to the old land surface below *(Fig. 27)*.

1849

Tunnel by John Merewether from the southern side into the centre of mound *(Fig. 27)*.

1867

Excavation to determine course of Roman Road *(Fig. 26)*. The location is marked by a deep scar near the base of the mound and is clearly visible as a small terrace on the south-east slope.

1886

Ten pits dug into fill of ditch surrounding the base of Silbury Hill and into the water storage extension to the west *(Fig. 26)*. The depth of the holes below the present surface varied between 4.6 metres to 6.4 metres at the base of the mound. In spite of a prolonged dry summer the water in the holes rose to within 2.4 metres of the top. It was suggested by the excavators that the ditch and surrounding low ground was meant to hold water.

1915

Sealed entrance to Merewether tunnel collapsed leaving a hole above the original entrance thus creating renewed access to the tunnel. A deep, vertical scar on the south side above the 1849 tunnel marks the site.

1922

Professor Flinders Petrie, the well known Egyptologist, made two large cuttings on south side of mound to search for a possible entrance to a passage or tomb chamber. Several smaller cuttings were also made to determine the natural chalk surface beneath the mound *(Fig. 26)*. It is interesting to note that Professor Petrie also expressed the opinion that the deep ditch surrounding the hill and the excavated extension to the west was meant to be filled with water and this may have been the reason for the unusual low-lying location of the mound.

1923

The new entrance caused by collapse of the 1849 Merewether tunnel sealed with a metal plate. The location is visible as a deep horizontal scar on south side of hill.

1934

Hole appears in the centre of hill top above the vertical shaft dug in 1776. It was filled in with chalk rubble but left a shallow depression on top.

1959

Resistivity survey of mound showed no results of hidden tomb or objects.

1963

Wire mesh laid into sunken undulating ground to stabilize the turf above the vertical shaft area.

1968

Resistivity survey to probe into the mound from the top. However, it proved unsuccessful due to the wire mesh buried in 1963.

1968

Two core drilling rigs were winched to the top of Silbury Hill. The 3 inch diameter cores showed that the base of the mound above the original land surface was heavily saturated with water and the bulk of the hill was made up of dumped chalk rubble.

1968/70

Professor Atkinson made a tunnel into the centre above Merewether entrance *(Fig. 27)*. Several cuttings were made on top of the hill to investigate the upper structure of the mound. Similar cuttings were also made at the base of the hill to examine the ditch fill and locate the original land surface.

2000

Large hole appears on top of hill due to further internal collapse of shaft and tunnels.

2000/03

Seismic surveys and coring down into old land surface. Stabilising top of collapsed shaft with chalk and polystyrene. The machinery and equipment required was transferred to the top by helicopter and removed again by the same means *(Fig. 28)*. The hill has been designated a *'Site of Special Scientific Interest'* (SSSI) and is 'out of bounds' to the public.

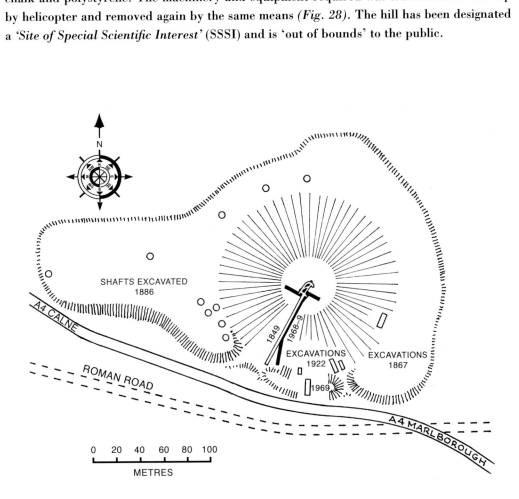

Fig. 26 *Plan view of tunnels and principal excavations within and around Silbury Hill.*

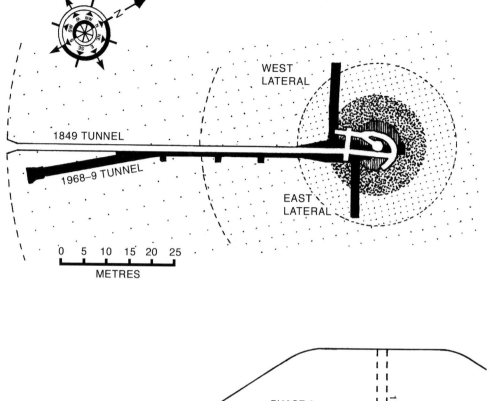

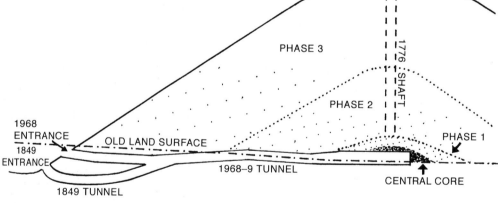

Fig. 27 *Plan and section of Silbury Hill showing vertical shaft and tunnels to centre of mound. The Duke of Northumberland in liaison with Colonel Drax sunk a shaft in 1776 – 77 from the centre at the top of the mound to the old land surface below. The work was carried out by Cornish miners. The tunnel dug in 1968 – 70 by Professor Richard Atkinson entered the hill above the collapsed entrance of the 1849 John Merewether tunnel and then followed the course of the original Merewether tunnel to the centre of the mound. An additional east and west lateral was excavated to probe into the mounds of Phase One and Phase Two.*

Fig. 28 *Helicopter removing equipment from the top of Silbury Hill in 2003 after finishing drilling operations. The fence on top of the hill has been removed but a new fence on the southern side adjacent to the A4 road has now been erected to prevent public access to the hill.*

SILBURY HILL CONSTRUCTION PHASES

CENTRAL CORE

Base 20 m diameter
1–2 m high
Surrounded by wattle fence
Shallow trench scooped out on valley floor

PHASE ONE

Base 35 m diameter
6 m high
Trench approx. 2 m deep x 8 m wide
Stabilized by chalk blocks and probably also Sarsen stones
Covered with turves
Phase One covered the Central Core and wattle fence

PHASE TWO

Base 75 m diameter
20 m high
Trench approx. 7 m deep x 14 m wide
Stabilized by chalk blocks and Sarsen stones
Covered with turves
Phase Two covered the mound of Phase One and the Central Core

PHASE THREE

Base 168 m diameter
37 m high
Six individual tiers 4–5 m high
Each tier stabilized with chalk blocks
Covered with turves as work progressed on each tier
Trench in places 9 m deep x 38 m wide
Large rectangular lake area towards west extending from 40 m to 160 m
Phase Three covered the mounds of Phase Two, Phase One and the Central Core
Top of finished mound 30 m diameter
Slopes approx. 30°

MARLBOROUGH MOUNT

Base 83 m diameter

19 m high

Top 31 m diameter

Width and depth of trench and original angle of slopes not known

HATFIELD BARROW

Base 70 m diameter

9 m high

Trench 28 m wide and 105 m in external diameter

Depth of trench and angle of slopes not known

BRIEF SUMMARY OF BRITISH CLIMATIC HISTORY FROM 8000 BC TO 450 AD.

8000 BC Pre-Boreal	Increasing warmth after melting of ice sheets.	Last of permanent ice gone from Britain.
7500 BC Pre-Boreal	Steady warming. Becoming drier. Rising sea levels.	Britain separated from Continent.
7000 BC Boreal	Further warming. Increased dryness. Short summers.	
6000 BC Boreal/ Early Atlantic	Remaining mild but becoming wetter.	
5000 BC Atlantic	Warm and damp. Cold winters.	
4000 BC Atlantic	Climatic optimum. 2° – 3° warmer than today. Winters less cold.	Windmill Hill settlements.
3500 BC Atlantic	Stable. Warm and dry. Long growing seasons.	Stonehenge phase 1.
3000 BC Sub-Boreal Late Atlantic	Warm and very dry. Mild winters.	Silbury Hill. Avebury. Palisade Enclosures. Marlborough Mount?
2500 BC Sub-Boreal	Less warm. Prolonged drier periods. Drought conditions.	Silbury Hill. Avebury. Palisade Enclosures. Marden Henge.
2000 BC Sub-Boreal	Decreasing warmth. Less dry.	Stonehenge phase 2. (Bluestones.) Stonehenge phase 3.
1000 BC Sub-Atlantic	Cool and wet.	
500 BC to 200 BC Later Sub-Atlantic	Deteriorating.	
200 BC to 450 AD	Warming up again. Long, dry periods.	Roman Settlements near Silbury Hill

Fig. 29

ADDITIONAL NOTES TO 'BRITISH CLIMATIC HISTORY 8000 BC TO 450 AD'.

Pre-Boreal   The first of the Post-Glacial climatic periods in Northern Europe succeeding the late-Glacial.

Boreal   A climatic zone characterized by long, cold, snowy winters and short summers. The term 'Boreal' meaning northern from the Latin 'Borealis'.

Atlantic period   (Climatic optimum). A term used to describe the warm and moist climatic phase with mean annual temperatures of 2 – 3 degrees higher than those of today.

Sub-Boreal   The early phase of decreasing warmth which succeeded the so-called climatic optimum. (Atlantic Period)

Sub-Atlantic   An expression used to describe the latter phase of decreasing warmth.

The dates shown in the table and the relevant climatic conditions for the immediate post glacial period in the British Isles differ greatly in the various records and should therefore be viewed with some caution. Regional variations of climate must also be taken into consideration.

Nevertheless, there is a broad consensus, substantiated by archeological evidence, that parts of the sub-boreal phase in the southern regions of Britain were dry to very dry with long periods of drought. Those seasonal arid conditions coincide with the construction of Silbury Hill, the Palisade Enclosures and the Hatfield Barrow within the Marden Henge. In view of its location and compelling circumstantial evidence it may be reasonable to assume that the Marlborough Mount fits also into the same time frame.

FURTHER READING

Sacred Mound Holy Rings.
Alasdair Whittle. Cardiff Studies in Archaeology 1997.
Published by Oxbow Books Oxford.

Archaeology in the Avebury Area.
A. B. Powell, M. J. Allen, I. Barnes.

Hidden Depths.
Isobel Geddes.
Published in 2000 by Ex Libries Press, Bradford-on-Avon, Wiltshire.

The Geology of Wiltshire.
R. S. Barron.
Published in 1976 by Moonraker Press, Bradford-on-Avon, Wiltshire.

Climate Through The Ages.
C. E. P. Brooks.
Published in 1970 by Constable & Co. Ltd., London.

Book Of The Weather.
Philip Eden.
Published in 2003 by Continuum, London.

Neolithic Britain.
Joshua Pollard.
Published in 2002 by Shire Publications, Risborough, Bucks.

The Environment Of Early Man In The British Isles.
John G. Evans.
Published in 1975 by Paul Eldeb & Co., London.

The Marlborough Mount.
David Field, Graham Brown, Andrew Crockett.
Wiltshire Archeological & Natural History Magazine Vol. 94 (2001)

Hatfield Barrow & Marden Henge.
Wiltshire County Council Sites and Monuments Records. File Reference: AA 70635/1

GLOSSARY

Aquifer	A permeable water-bearing reservoir rock supplying water to wells and springs.
Blue Stones	A type of igneous rock from the Preseli Mountains in south-west Wales.
Catchment Area	A region which drains rainwater or other precipitation into a river or stream.
Chalk Promontory	A chalk spur projecting into a vale.
Coombe	In southern England a hollow or short valley penetrating into the Chalk Downs.
Cretaceous	A period in the Earth's history from 145 million to 65 million years ago, following the Jurassic period.
Cross-bedding	Internal laminations within a deposit inclined at an oblique angle to the main bedding-plane.
Duricrust	A hard layer formed in upper soil horizons by the evaporation of mineral-saturated groundwater in a semi-arid climate.
Haematite	Ferric iron oxide, an iron ore.
Headward Retreat	The cutting back of a valley or gully by the eroding action of water from a spring.
Ice Age	A geological period in which ice-sheets and glaciers covered large areas of the earth's surface. The last ice age started 1.5 million years ago and finished about 10000 years ago.
Induration	The hardening of soft sediments through the deposition of minerals which act as cement on or within the surface layers.
Marl	A fine grained sedimentary rock in the form of a clay or mudstone.
Molluscs	An invertebrate animal having a hard calcareous shell, i.e. snails.
Neolithic	A term adapted from the Greek meaning 'New Stone age' from 4400 BC to 2500 BC and followed by the 'Bronze Age' 2500 BC to 800 BC.
Patina	A surface film produced by chemical weathering of minerals within a rock.
Permafrost	A ground that is frozen all the time. A shallow layer of surface soil may thaw during the summer.

Pyrite The form of iron sulphide. A brass-yellow mineral with a bright metallic lustre often mistaken for gold, hence the common name *'Fool's Gold'*.

Quartz A hard, glass-like mineral consisting of crystalline silica.

Quartzite An extremely hard resistant sandstone rock consisting primarily of Quartz grains cemented by silica.

Radiocarbon Dating A method of dating rocks or organic material by measuring the proportion of the C^{14} isotope which breaks down at a known rate.

Red Loam An easily worked permeable soil deriving its red colour from the presence of iron oxide.

Resistivity Survey An electrical method of geophysical exploration which may indicate some obscured feature below ground.

Seismic Survey The investigation of subterranean rock structures by the reflection of seismic or shock waves.

Silica A silicon dioxide of which quartz is the most common form.

Silicification Replacement of structures within organic or inorganic material by the introduction of silica from groundwater or igneous sources.

Soil Creep The very slow movement of surface soil down a slope.

Spring Sapping The erosional process around the point where a spring issues from the ground.

Spring-head Alcoves Headward retreat of a steep-sided gully formed by the eroding action of water from a spring.

Spring-line A linear zone where the water table intersects the ground surface at the foot of a slope or escarpment.

Tertiary The period in the Earth's history from 65 million years to 2 million years ago, following the Cretaceous period.

Water table The upper surface of groundwater in an aquifer, a water-bearing rock.

INDEX